Crossing the Carpathians

Carmen Bugan was born in Romania, and has lived in the United States and Ireland. She now lives in Oxford.

CARMEN BUGAN

Crossing the Carpathians

Oxford*Poets*

CARCANET

First published in Great Britain in 2004 by
Carcanet Press Limited
Alliance House
Cross Street
Manchester M2 7AQ

Copyright © Carmen Bugan 2004

The right of Carmen Bugan to be identified as the author of this work
has been asserted by her in accordance with the
Copyright, Designs and Patents Act of 1988
All rights reserved

A CIP catalogue record for this book is available from the British Library
ISBN 1 903039 68 1

The publisher acknowledges financial assistance from Arts Council England

Typeset by XL Publishing Services, Tiverton

For my mother, father, brother and sister

Acknowledgements

Many thanks to the following publications for including slightly modified versions of poems in this collection: *Oxford Poets 2001: An Anthology* (Manchester, Carcanet Press), *Big Scream* (Grandville, Nada Press), *Cyphers* (Dublin, ELO Press), *HazMat Review* (New York, Clevis Hook Press), *The Oxonian Review of Books* (Balliol College, Oxford), *PN Review*, *The Reader* (Oxford University Poetry Society), *The Tabla Book of New Verse 2004* (University of Bristol), *West 47* (Galway Arts Centre). Very early versions of some of these poems were privately printed in two chapbooks, *between us* (1993) and *at the borders* (1995). Thanks are also due to the editors of the Balliol College student magazine *Scrawl* and the online publication www.dublinwriters.org.

Contents

On the side of forgetting

for my grandmother Anghelina

I

We stood in the main doorway
According to the custom of important days
(Usually marked by the village priest
With holy water dripping from dry basil
But now recorded in the slow turn of hinges):
Come back, you said, *I will*, I said.

You stored the coffers with my dowry
And we walked to the station before dawn.

The moon whitened the crossing of dirt roads
Spread like open palms.

II

After I learned the new language
And abandoned the old one,
I practised pronouncing new words
And felt new in their newness.

When leaves turned their backs in storms
I sat imagining that I was a child by the sea
Whistling through a flute made of cornstalk.

Once I saw you in the crisscross of afternoon sunlight,
Lighting a candle under stained glass —
A heart beating under the ribs of a city
You will never see.

The church orchestra practised for Evensong
And something in me, like the breath released
From the throat of the flute, escaped:
I mattered to no one there.

III

This morning I awoke to the sound
Of birds inside the yellow of gorse bushes,
The hands of hills are in the sea,
Tory Island is a boat without sails.
You whisper to me from hawthorns and hazels,
The earth will remember you.

Your wooden cross appears to me
Through the rain washing the cemetery.
I want to walk around your grave
Three times, light incense and a candle
Inside the rusted bottomless bucket
Lodged in the earth next to your head.

In the silent country

When the hens climbed the tree to sleep and the dog was let loose in
                                                                the yard,
When their children went to bed, she covered the windows
In the doors with towels and hung the yellow blanket over the curtain rod.
He went outside, around the farthest corner of the house, dug the
                                                                typewriter
From its hole, then from the garage brought a stack of papers
Hidden behind tools in a box. They locked the room.

Both sat at the large oak table and put on gloves to hide fingerprints.
Each night, one by one, hundreds of pages darkened with communal
                                                                demands:
Hot water, electricity, freedom of speech, freedom to worship, freedom
                                                                to assemble.
Their arms smelled of fresh ink and the room was the sound of struck keys
Between two breaths. Not one star looked inside, but the wind joined
                                                                the hush
Of shuffled paper. Before the rooster broke the news of dawn, he put
                                                                the typewriter

In its white crate and buried it in the ground at the back of the house.
She stacked the leaflets in boxes with beans on top – same beans for months,
Wrinkled and dry like old thumbs. With the towels back in the closet
And the blanket down, the room returned to order, quiet and dark like
                                                                the street.
They kissed the children in their sleep. Posing as farmers, they left for
                                                                distant towns
Where he filled mailboxes while she watched for informers and police.

Hues of mornings changed with seasons, but the early sun
Spilled light over his face, over her hands holding the map.
At times, when they stopped to wash out the sleep with cold water, he
                                                                could see
The dark of her eyes. Fists met at the market and in the store,
Churches were demolished, and no one said a word:
Those waiting in eternal lines, or those who saw the crosses kneel

In the rubble of saints and chalices. When they slept, words
Rose from the stacks and they breathed them as they were on papers:
Hot water, electricity, freedom of speech, freedom to worship, freedom
to assemble.
They retraced in dreams each step: typewriter in the ground,
Papers behind the tools, gloves in the cupboard, the dark entryways
Where the words went, someone looking at them through a crack in
the door.

Every night the words replaced them – *her pale skin, her long brown hair.*
They whispered into the sleep of others, in the silent country.

Portrait of a family

When the strangers walked into the house,
Took the paintings off the walls, and
Sealed off the rooms with red wax,

Part of this poem listened in a hospital. A woman's milk
Fed the words she couldn't say into her child's mouth.
For seven months the strangers stayed in the house.

Someone tied the hands of the man
Who inflamed the centre of the capital with protest
While they took the paintings off the walls.

A few lines cowered in the grass, outside the windows,
With the neighbours who watched the girl answering questions
To the strangers who settled into the house.

And yet someone followed her sister on the streets
And photographed her pure black eyes,
Unsuspecting in the paintings on the walls.

Now that the strangers have left the house
The poem would like to know:
Can it place once more the paintings on the walls,
Will the son tell the secrets of his mother's milk,
Will the handcuffs come off the man's hands,
Will the girl stop answering questions,
Will her sister burn the photographs?

The demonstration

I remember the night my father left
Filling a bag with leaflets and tying the placards
On top of the car: 'We Demand the Trial of the Ceausescu Family
For Crimes Against Humanity, Usury and Economic Downfall.'
I complained about the boiled cabbage.
Please come and lock the gates. Tell them nothing.
I fell asleep on the kitchen sofa listening to Radio Free Europe.

In Bucharest he placed the placards on the front and back of the car.
He drove through traffic on the main street.
People came out of the stores shouting.
Buses and trams stopped, emptied, let him pass.
He threw leaflets with the left hand, drove with the right hand.
Ah, it was glorious! The flag of his country draped round his chest.
The portrait of the dictator decorated with black ribbons.

In a hospital, Dad's only son was born –
Mother held his bluish body wrapped in white cloth
At the window.

Thousands saw him being pulled from the car.
Watched him between armed soldiers.
None of his countrymen said a word.

Fertile ground

I was pruning tomato plants when they came to search
For weapons in our garden;
They dug the earth under the chickens, bell peppers,
Tiny melons, dill, and horseradishes.

I cried over sliced eggplants
Made one with the dirt,
Over fresh-dug earth and morning glories.

Their shovels uncovered bottles
With rusted metal caps – sunflower cooking oil
My father kept for 'dark days', purchased in days equally dark.
Their eyes lit – everyone got a bottle or two –
A promise for their families' meals.

And when the oil spilled on the ground, shiny over crushed tomatoes
They asked me about weapons we might have kept.
'Oil,' I said: 'You eat and live.
This alone makes one dangerous.'

The first visit

The family went inside cement walls
In the centre of the town,
Stood inside metal gates
In the centre of the prison,
And waited. Hours swelled
Like the shadows of passing black trucks
Loaded with *criminals*.

When they finished shaving him,
After they covered the wounds on his head with a cap,
There was a rumble of chains and keys.
His wife and children were taken to the visiting room:
'Twenty minutes,' the guard said.

Twenty minutes in August each year
Twenty minutes –
A mouth full of suffering,
Words swollen by microphones
Sank into the thick wall of glass
Between us.

Through two rooms, through two square holes in the walls
The little boy said: 'Daddy, I thought I'd bring you some apples.'

The divorce

Before they brought him to the courtroom, they gave him three apples:
'Your wife sent you these.' He cradled each apple in the cup of his hands,
The smoothness of their skin became the cheeks of each child.

Inside the courthouse there was a quiet opening and closing of doors.
A crowd of people was chanting his name under the windows.
When the door opened, I saw his bare feet in brown shoes.

His children held each other tight against the wall.
Their breaths, white with cold, were rising towards the ceiling.
They listened for the voices of their parents.

When the divorce was over, he was allowed to see them:
They kissed his chained hands, promised to be good, let their tears fall
On his prison uniform with his own, all three of them burying him.

How I wished we could hide him with our bodies and take him home!
The Securitate peeled us off him. But we were the apple seeds left to grow
In the sound of his chains on the cement floor.

Exorcism

'Drink three mouthfuls
Of this hot wine
While you think
Of the man with the axe
Aiming at your throat
When you turn in bed.'

Nu mai ai putere asupra mea deacum inainte.

'In this pot
I melt lead
While I think
Of the man with the axe
Aiming at your throat
Just as you drink the wine.'

Nu mai ai putere asupra mea deacum inainte.

In the wine
The lead hissed;
He raised
The axe
To his shoulder,
His body twisted
Turned
Swelled
Froze.
Red drops
Fell
From his head
And evil eyes.

Nu mai ai putere asupra mea deacum inainte.

You no longer have power over me
I cried all the way home
After I paid the witch twenty *lei* –
All the money we had for food
That week.

Stories for the night

The family sat in the kitchen again for the first time in years;
The white table filled with plates of polenta, meat, and goat's cheese,
Glasses of water halfway empty, a tiny red carnation in a vase at the centre.

The father smiled sadly at his children from the head of the table:
'Don't ask me things before going to bed,
These are not your grandmother's stories.'
He dropped his hands to his knees and looked at each of them:

'One night they woke me up and beat me,
The fat officer hit me over the left ear; I can't hear well since.
They tied me up and hung me on the wall, my hands chained behind
my back,
Toes barely touched the floor. I stood there for thirty-six hours.

One of the three men from my cell died:
We propped him up, told the guards he was alive
So we could have his bread and water.
After some time he smelled bad, rats were eating too much of him
And we gave him away.

A man tied to a wheel
A man pinned to a wall
Shards of glass in our soup
That's how it was there.'

Confession to my son

I signed the paper Son, I did:
You are not blood of my blood
Flesh of my flesh,
You will not cradle my head in death.
Forgive me Son: I told them to kill you.

I never showed you the fracture on my head.
Your mother keened in the yard –
White hair down to her waist,
Hands around her hips – she wept, and wept.
My hand was put to the paper.
I thought my eyes will never meet yours
And these words will never meet you.
They said they will demolish the house.
The day was as beautiful as if nothing happened.
I imagined pieces of the sitting room
Small enough to fit in my palm,
Blue and warm, worn with years.
I remember us both polishing wood for the closets,
And the way you hid field mice under your shirt,
'Look how my heart is beating, Daddy,' you'd say…
I don't know when I woke up
But I was singing:

I lost a son
A son I lost
By my hand.

I lost a son
By my hand
My son.

Taking leave

You take my hand between rough fingers
And we cross the ocean on the map to America.
I think of days left for you to have wine and walnuts,
To feed pigeons in the yard with corn grains,
Of one more spring when you will walk the palms
Of your hands over the yellow bed of tulips.

Sitting on a chair in front of the house
Even through the haze of Alzheimer's you know
This leave-taking is the final one – and how are we
To stretch this moment so far that it will last a lifetime?
We, who go, stand in front of you waiting for blessings
From your blue, confused, wet eyes.

'Make me an altar before you go,
In the kitchen, on top of the cupboard.
On your grandmother's crochet tablecloth,
With grapes made of fabric, put the icons of St Mary
And St Nicholas. Then light the oil lamp, my child.
After you leave I'll pray for you there.'

Around us, neighbours and family weep with the weeping of funerals,
Two dumb girls plead with us not to go,
The crowd is astonished at their garbled words.
And only when Mother starts pounding on Dad's chest
Overcome with the madness of leaving everything,
You stand up: 'It's your duty to go,' you say.
The crowd walks us to the gate, the car, a dog barks,
Birds sing. It is October.
Alone, you are left in the chair, warmed only by the sun.

The train station at the border

At Moravita the last officer opened each suitcase
And turned each pocket inside out.
He felt the lining of coats, his thievish hands
Fondled and fondled.

It was words he took, words
Hidden between socks and underclothes in a blue notebook:
Condemned for propaganda against the socialist regime
This day of September 1983.
While passengers watched, the family was escorted out
Onto the stone platform where the day woke up cold.

All day and all night,
They sat on a stone bench in a stone station.
The father was angry with the final body search.
His face, flushed and desperate,
Tried to regain dignity as he stepped
From the stone office into the stone hall.
Through small windows
October went on colouring trees.
The army hounds paced around the station with the soldiers.
The little boy never said he was hungry,
The mother made a bed for him
Out of suitcases and winter coats;
There he slept without dreams.
His parents and two sisters
Paced inside the stone station at the border
Without a glass of water, without a word.

Grand Rapids, Michigan

Father repeats his own name aloud as if to remember it:
Sheepskin coat, blood-shot eyes, one suitcase,
His carries his age and his language on his tongue.

Mother gathers us around her:
I still see on her face the green lights on the platform in Bucharest,
The arm of the conductor lifting to *Go!*

When we crossed the frontier
We drank quietly from a flask of plum brandy:
I still don't know what each of us was thinking.

Someone carries a sign with our name written on it,
We don't know him but embrace him
And let him drive us through driving snow

In exile

…and I've been searching for home
ever since the train whistled in darkness.

Home

In last night's dream gladioli grew wild around the house
Queens-of-the-night crashed through walls
And the remains of the windowsills were overtaken
By tall while lilies and blue irises.
The roses we grew for preserves strangled the front door.

I was sitting next to the poplar grown through the roof
When I saw a man hanging smoked fish under the eaves.
My grandparents were having a meal of bread, onion, and water;
They were talking about bringing the corn to the mill
And threshing the beanstalks in the yard.

From the beans, the smell of summer.
I saw the sticks we made out of oak branches,
I remembered how we sat in the circle,
The dust from the stalks as we beat them –
Something like the sound of galloping horses.

They carried on with the meal. Then they sifted wheat.
I saw them walk right past me. They loaded the cart.
And I thought I heard my name in the throat of a gladiolus.

For Sorin

It was never a festival
Of chrysanthemums,
Holding each other in parks.

Never an oath on St Mary's painting,
Ready to abandon words,
Rolling in the grass at night.

Never love-making –
The still wet hair,
Cards I sent from Trieste.

Never building a house.
But I imagined we'd live in the mountains
With peasants, getting drunk,

Chopping wood in winters,
Riding horses in summers,
Betting on the weather.

Ann Arbor

Sidewalks burn my shoes,
Peruvian musicians play and dance
In a circle in their dark sweat,
Packs of people walk around,
Restless sky above it all.

In front of this brick building
Sun makes gold with your hair;
We sit on small chairs in the piazza,
Your eyes make soft outlines, contours
Around me.

You take a handful of dirt
And watch it run through your fingers,
The smile on your face sits like a restless
Sparrow on its nest.
How deep the slice of sky is turning
Inside my chest.

For you

I saw you and I spared nothing.
I turned twenty dancing in
Your blue shorts at the beach in Saugatauck.

We wrote vows one sleepless night
And you stole me away in a carriage of roses
After our wedding in two languages.

My head slept on the right side of your chest
And dreamed the purpose of love into your heart
While you, afraid that I'd stop breathing, watched me.

Return to sound

At the Black Sea I touched a broken shell, its soft edges,
Fish and algae brushed against its white glow,
    Waves threw it on the sand
    Where it remembered the pulse of the depths.

At one edge of the house I turn eastwards,
I curl my palms and press them against my ears:
    All is quiet, only the blood returns to me like the sea
    And the sea moves the sand.

Sitting with a hurricane lamp in America

You return as I light this lamp
      In a yard you've never known,
            Between stars and this light
            I also come home.

At the foot of the star cross
      You are the darting light
            Dante's Cacciaguida
            Brighter than the rest.

To study medicine, you spent nights
      With a small candle
            Under the kitchen bed
            With tall wooden legs

And a hay-stuffed mattress,
      Flowers pressed
            Like fragments of ballads
            In the brown cotton sack.

God gave me the candle in a dream –
      Gold halo around his head
            And eyes like Alpine pools –
            Many years ago.

That August afternoon
      Floating in sleep
            The wax burned
            The back of my fingers:

'Don't let it fall. This is the candle of your life.'

I am hungry for the raspberries
      Next to the coal mine
            Where you liked to return
            To ask things hidden in your skull.

I walk on granite stone
      Wanting not to feel
            The void of your death
            Because I wasn't there.

At her funeral

for my grandmother

Villagers dressed in black lay bridges of cloth
From the living room to the carriage
And walk the coffin on their shoulders,
Over the threshold,
Over the bed of chrysanthemums
She had looked at in the early mornings.

The mourners put their hands together
Under the black ribbons above the doors,
And sing of her eyebrows turning into moss
Her eyes turning into violets,
Her bones turning into flutes.

The priest leads the cortège to the church
With the book and three boys carrying scarf-flags.
They stop at every street corner
To make prayers of return into humid earth.

Here, in the horse-drawn carriage
She is a bride crossing the gate to the cemetery
Behind a trail of incense and songs,
A wooden cross, and a box filled with bread.

Hundreds of oak leaves whisper in the sun.
Her soul, like a vapour,
Joins the afternoon light
From mounds of flowers and lit candles.

Doorways

for my aunt Sáftica

In the depths of the night I want to come inside
Your house through the white peeling door,

The one with the window on which you placed
A hand-woven shawl with patterns of nasturtiums.

But on the other side of the door where you waved years ago
I fear that you have woven me into the knowledge of a winter rug

With all the reds and yellows you had thread for
While I stayed hidden in my silence.

Leac na cumhaidg

There is no cure for homesickness.

I lean on the yard gate and I am glad that it still groans.
Someone put geraniums in the windows to the veranda.
The door handle fits familiar in my palm, as if I never left.
In the hallway the aroma of red apples bursts into me.

Without parents I return: I want to cure my homesickness alone.

In the kitchen, still the double bed next to the stove.
Through the window, the altar side of the church
Where Mary and Joseph walk in a painting,
The judgement happens in another and God is benevolent.

The room returns to me the childhood years:
The smell of baking pumpkins from grandfather's garden,
The microphones set in the curtain rods,
Dad's postcards from prison: 'I am fifty, make a cake for me.'

The sunflower oil lamp is gone from the eastern wall,
So is the white kitchen table where we had our first meal when Dad
returned.
The newly painted walls are accustomed to the silence
Of us not being there: this is a return to something else.

There is no cure for homesickness.

'Leac na cumhaidg': the stone that is said to cure homesickness, near Gartan Lough,
Ireland.

I drink with you

for my aunt Sáftica

When you knew that I was leaving
You bought me a pair of red shoes;
I left them in Florence with the memory of your hands.
You were unsure when you said 'So you'll dance and forget.'
October was pale in a bouquet of chrysanthemums.
For every year that I was gone you buried in the ground
One crimson bottle of wine. I never knew this –
How you felt when you gathered the sweetness of autumn
And hoped that its magic would call me back.
Now I touch the corners of your black scarf,
The white hair of your widow-braids. I kiss your hands
Which rest on the wine-stained tablecloth.

Emilia

When he corners Emilia in the kitchen
     And strikes her because the house is cold,
The thin white curtain in the small window
     Breathes with the air of his arm, moving.
Next to the stove is a bundle of twigs
     She had stolen from the nearby woods.

He smells like coal and vodka,
     His face is the black which never washes off.
Today she slept with the baker for a loaf of bread
     She carried home under her armpit to keep warm;
She breaks it for her husband and her daughter
     And gathers the crumbs in a cloth napkin.

At night she bends over the family well
     To bring the stars closer.

At three in the morning, she peels
     Frost-bitten potatoes, opens a jar of eggplants,
Makes linden tea to keep in the cupboard for medicine.
     When the breakfast is ready, she hums to herself.

In the afternoon the alarm shrieks over the mountain,
     She takes her daughter to see who has died;
He is brought in a coal cart from the depths,
     Head crushed, arms severed, both palms open.

The song of the dead grows on her cracked lips
     On the path to the garden, past the stork's nest,
Just as she rehearsed it from the beginning
     Of her life.

Walking by the Atlantic at low tide

One wave with the breath in its throat
Thrown back by shore wind

Whispers like you: propped in bed
Hair soft and white, spread on the pillow.

Crossing the Carpathians with you

for my mother

Mountains and us clothed
In soft white fog,
Suddenness of cliffs.

You and I carve walking sticks,
Bursts of sun dust
Thousands of yellow and violet flowers.

Red and white polka-dot
Mushrooms among trees,
Strong smell of ferns and cones.

Stones in pots on our backs
Warnings to black bears,
We gather forget-me-nots.

Distant curves
Of snow and peaks
In the white of the moon.

Shepherds' rain fast and thin
We empty the boots of water,
A bear licks out pots.

I know what it means to go
Anywhere with you: you are
The moss on which I sleep.

Sleeping apple

I want to sleep the sleep of the apples
                                    Lorca

She dreams of how constellations
Of apples turn in their sleep
Towards stars in the silence
Of the orchard.

I know she dreams:
She glows in the basket
Nestled among blushing sisters.

The day we decided we would lie

I buried the blown bloom of white lilac
Into the heart of spring, straight
In the middle of that unacknowledged pact.

And it woke up inside the gust of wind
Repeating its incomprehensible grief
In the window of first winter without you.

I now send it to you in your country:
Don't tell me what you do with white lilacs on your doorstep,
On your table, on your windowsill, in your hands…

By the lamp, burning

Today I untangled a butterfly from my hair –
By this light I imagine him again
Yellow tangled in yellow –

For three days now I've spoken to no one.
Only fireflies light my way back to camp.

I have been aware of you:
The never touches beside the tent,
The torn off pages with the way
I did not take.

Cursing the tongue

Tonight I am cursing the tongue for breaking the eternal
Inside the fort of Hornhead, when it thought it knew
From eyes and lips and the white of bog cotton
That we were always going to live by foxgloves
Or at least by their memory, but in our house of dreams.

When the sun went to Michigan
Leaving only the silhouette of Tory Island,
You spread blooms of heather in my hair and looked at me
Through the unsheltered windows of the fort, and
When our hands held, waves lifted the ocean to us.

Now I keep a photograph in which I walk away
And one in which a swan is as white as the emptiest pain.
Tonight I curse the tongue
For it invented belief in love which lasts.

Lullaby

Gentle, gentle my love,
Let this ease off
Like dying in sleep.

Quiet, quiet my love,
Let us part cold
Like the moon on the wall.

Last night you tasted
The salt of the sea on my cheeks:
Let it be fluid like that.

Gentle, gentle my love,
Let me not know
When we make love last.

Quiet, quiet my love,
I'll go quiet and gentle,
I'll go like light.

Memories

We have been inhabited by the sound of these mandolins
On islands and coasts which *still weep* with light.

I remember clearly the sound of your voice calling me
From the doorstep, and your palm hiding mine

In something as *absolute*
As my drive in a car filled with our years thrown in boxes.

I was always the journey and point of return, the place
Where you ended up, and made a sort of music, smiling.

Dry-throat, empty-mouth repeating farewells
And night dreams rehearse the same promises:

That you will meet me at those crossroads
Where we buy the wine of forgetting with the coin of the moon.

In the middle of eternity

Without you I skip stones on the Thames
Stone-skipping days – sad throwers, lover throwers,
Skilled throwers of skipping stones –
Timeless creatures at edges of rivers…

Each time I call your name at the end of love and forgetting
I am part of the eternal ending of love and of forgetting.
Never alone, never absolute,

I utter in the vastness of being
The humdrum of the riverbank:
Your name escaped from my mouth into the air
Is a stone-skipping arch on the river's face.

This spring

While she uproots blooming irises from the backyard
Where they grow for no one
And brings them to the flower bed next to the road,
Gusts of wind and sun blind and lose her.

She digs with her fingers to feel the reality of soil
Not as harsh as the pain of letting go
Or as otherworldly as the bird's nest which
She knocks over with her shoulder.

But she looks for that softness and warmth
That will be a sort of home – after death.

The father wobbles in his sandals towards the flowers
Thinking of the image of his heart on the monitor –
A muscle the size of his fist flickering with the weight of light.

She plants a row of irises on the side of house and he smiles
At fragrant violet and white petals unfolding:
'In July we'll have gladioli and next year
Let's get lots of colours, lots of colours.'

She tells him that the peonies and geraniums and roses and tiger lilies
Grow so strongly it must be a good sign: he will get better, she says.

This is the hour when there is only time for
Delicate colours around the grey house, the locust trees in the yard
From which they take armfuls of blossoms and bring them in
And fill the rooms with the white scent of blown spring.

For my father

You sign your full name with a stick on the freshly poured
Path of cement: the end of the last letter returns to your first name
In the wet dust. Around, a slew of peonies
Hurry to bloom before the bluebells, before you plant them.

You surprise me with dill seeds from Grandmother
That you kept since our last trip home.
You brought her in this soil and now we are together
Through plants we touched in different countries.

Remember? A cart full of red and white grapes at the head
Of our vineyard, red wine pressed years before,
Goat's cheese and tomatoes spread under the oak tree
And horses let loose for children whose voices ripened the earth.

★

I have the picture in which you crossed yourself in front of St Mary's
icon at Vatra.
It was the first week of chemotherapy when we had the service with
Seven candles and seven prayers and seven readings from the Gospels.
Seven times we walked to the altar where the priest painted crosses with
holy oil

On our cheeks, on our foreheads, and the backs of our hands. For we
must sin
With our minds, hurt others with our hands, and carry our shame on
our faces.
So we try to redeem ourselves with our minds, and hands, and clean our
cheeks.
I look at your pale profile, at your balding head in front of those candles

And ask what the mother in red and her child in white, carefully placed
In the whitest of wood frames, will do for you.
We cried with you: Mother, I, and a congregation of exiles
Dreaming their own into the smoke of the censer.

★

We are small gardens in strange places, small voices –
Prayers weakening with age and heavy accents hammering wrong
                                                    syllables:
Does God understand us in English or our own language still?

You choose the path with handwriting that marks your name and year
And I carry your garden in my head, along with the memory of you and
                                                    Mother
Embracing on the doorstep the day we received the news:
In the months to come what binds us is the most silent of prayers,
                                                    unuttered still.

Flight dream

At three in the afternoon I slung
The hiking boots over the rucksack
And left Oxford in a pool of June sun.

Crowds of motorcycles in Poole Harbour,
Through narrow streets, boats and seagulls:
Half industrial, half dreamy, this is not my place.

Ten o'clock finds me tense in a yellow room
Caught dreaming between two islands
Or rather imagining my head in your palms.

Handfast Point

After I saw the peacock on the sand,
Proud and dispossessed
Of its blue by the sunlit tide,

I thought of you, miles on,
Past the pottery beach,
After reeds, willows and birch:

You, of course, are the one
Who would understand
Cursing and releasing

The heart, white chalk
Like the rock of Old Harry,
With the blue hand of sea.

Black Head Ledges

This is the safe white room with a sea window
And rain after sun, a badger among bluebells.
My hosts tell me of their travels over *palinka*

And Hungarian wine from the Valley of Egar.
This is how I arrived here: when the clouds
Came like premonitions over the Black Head Ledges,

I lost faith and pressed on, weight on mind and body.
Then the sun returned and shone over Osmington
More like a lighthouse beam than a promise.

The distance between the path and the edge,
Sure footing and falling under weight of backpack
Opened with the hours between cliffs and sky – in long silence.

The second spring

for my father

I hasten to say to myself that it is March and you survived
And for fear of losing you, I play music over

The telephone and I waltz with you across the sea on 'Blue Danube'
Only as the two of us would, after we lost and found ourselves again.

I only fear for your life now in dreams: when I awake, you are reachable.
Oh, Dad, spring here arrived unexpectedly: one day

Thames flooded the snowdrops: what was left of the meadow
Was taken up with daffodils and violets and scatterings of green.

Windspit

Beyond the Dancing Ledge the salt breeze widens
And whispers into caves, but its sound at times
Hurls itself underground, then rises just as a hum

To where my feet, blistered and determined
Meet the old path. I search again with
Sea-tasting hair in dry mouth –

The weight of winspit, wishspit, windspit
Love which opens to love of sorts:
Pub table, drenched clothes, white cliffs;

At the end of today's walk over the sound
Of sea under the path, sudden soft
Explosions through gaps and tunnels, underfoot.

Moorings

We shall leave what has not been said alone.
All I know is the strength of your arms and that
You seem to anchor the side of the room where you stand.

Or how you carried me home last night,
Across rooms and road and doors,
It almost *sounded* like hushed sparrow wings

Or like white sails on steady-wind seas.
The voice on the telephone, your smiles,
Moorings and mornings of the most silent of loves.

Poem without a name

There is no life except in the word of it
Wallace Stevens

The rain talked all day in the window of Sunday
But it did not interrupt the morning game of chess,
Game of silent traps and awkward laughter.

Of course we did not notice it at lunch
Because we kept busy preparing food, speaking with friends –
An eyelash fell on my right cheek but you were briefly away
When I made the wish and blew it on the floor.

I only began to hear the rain in the afternoon:
It talked into my lips until, drenched and washed, I returned from the walk
Carrying rain in the folds of my palms.

All day the rain said that you will return to the other end of the earth
Without a word in the life of this love. We went for dinner with
An umbrella and I stopped listening.

At the window

Wet leaf slapped itself against the glass,

You turned directly to my mouth in the crowd

Then slid down

Lowered yourself to my waist

Leaving the mark of its width along the window.

Until, transparent, I bore your kiss.

Past solitude

Breakfast of mackerel at a table facing foxgloves
Then luck of low tide: so I slid on boulders,
Threaded a small footpath through mud, all the while

Balancing backpack and weight on boots.
When I thought that river Char opens its mouth into the sea,
I regretted the blackness of my words to you

And hoped that tides would keep cleaning them from me.
From Charmouth to Chideock I walked on the motorway
And from there to Seatown, thatch-roofed cottages and fields of lambs.

All the way to West Bay it was cliff-top to bottom-of-hill,
Deep green under a grey sky and breath-labour.
I am a snail, moving slowly, watchful and regretful at times.

Here, at the window, after gravel beach which led
To golden cliffs in which I stuck my fingers at the end
Of solitude, I paint myself with the dusk of Sunday.

Lyme Regis

It is now two years later, close to the ice
Of my birthday, one spent half-alone –
When at the edge of a different water

I turn, reach for your hand, and
Sense your smile warming my cheek:
It's as if only hours ago our palms left each other.

To my left, where you usually were,
A seagull stands on a basket of flowers
And the emptiness empties itself into waves.

I run in the downpour, uphill to my hotel,
Only to learn that I forgot our address,
And know that a postcard won't help.

Abbotsbury

Eype Mouth, Burton Freshwater, Burton Beach, Cogden Beach,
And yellow, yellow rape patches folded in soft hills which
Kneel, golden and wrinkled, towards the speaking sea.

Then Chesil Beach and boots and blue pool surprising
The eye with its stillness – rhythm of gravel walk and waves,
An afternoon of intense heat and colours in the heart of silence.

Imagine a bride, wild with waiting for first night:
She throws handfuls of roses in hidden valleys
Where they take root in the stone of houses.

That is Abbotsbury. She goes to pray
At St Nicolas's Abbey up on the hill and buries her past
In the hip of the cemetery which faces the Fleets.

And she raises a thousand swans now nesting
And she turns her flock of lambs in the sunlight.
I walk over her body, dream-eyed.

A house of stone

for Mark and Ella

In the village where I was born, we wish
A house of stone to shelter the heart of the marriage

So here too, I wish you
Obstinate, strong love, unyielding and unending.

May you be in reach of each other when all seems lost,
May your tears and your smiles happen always face to face.

When you imagine that you have shared everything
May you know that you still have the rest of your lives
To do all of it again and again.

But now listen to the hurry of bells and
Look how petals of roses about the vineyard

Bring you the words, 'husband' and 'wife':
First words in your house of stone.

Blindness, beside another war

She flew into the sky reflected on the window
And stopped singing against the eight o'clock news, forever.
Was it a navigation mistake or the fault of the glass
Hiding all things in the room behind
The paleness of the winter sun at the tree line?

Then, as if you did not hear the crash of claws and feathers,
You sent lovely Russian songs underneath and through
Your half-opened door, oblivious in the wires
Of the stereo, (straight from the Urals, I imagine
Or maybe Norinskaia or Voronetz…)

Lately, such strange things keep happening –
Messages arrive from the end of world
Fastened tight in the belly of an accordion,
And everything looks as clear and deceiving as a mirror
Or a shut window into which one might fly.

March 2003

Under Magdalen Tower, with you

Spring rites
Ancient bells:

A prayer and
Two songs.

The space into

It is the sound of the *flamenco* guitar
Hypnotic through midday flooded paths

Swollen Thames like the eyes of a lover
Into morning hours finite with end of hope.

No: it is the absence of you that seeps through the wall,
Hollow like the bone of the magpie into the order of cleaned path.

That sound of you on the other side – material and daydream –
Quiet footsteps,

The *reverberation* of your voice which tells me you hear
When I return.

After seven years, for the unearthing of your body

Tomorrow they will open your grave:
Your bones will sound against each other,

The voice of your hills lulls frozen grass
To rest, to rest, to rest in peace.

The priest will chant *Vesnica Pomenire*,
The family will feast on pilaf and grape leaves.

This Saturday your soul will take another journey;
I write to wish you light, from here

Where the moon is stuck full to the window
White, unmerciful, sinking in curtains.

All night above the grave, everyone will sit with you
Drinking the wine you pressed for this wake.

The church choir – all your friends – will sing,
And Grandmother will be there, in death as in life.

She waited for you nine years, dreaming in the ground
Just as you waited, lighting incense at her head;

In spring, when you cleared the weeds from her grave
You thought of lying next to her, close to the train tracks.

'I like the train whistling' you said once
While we picked violets in the cemetery.

Since you died, you have returned to me three times:
Once you were in my husband's dream,

Once we sat on the balcony with a wind-lamp,
And last, you held my hand in a poem.

Grandfather, I am in Ireland now, and tonight
They say the two worlds meet and speak to each other.

Arrive in a dream or vision;
The fire is burning, I lit three candles

There are prayers turning in my sleep
And I listen to songs I learned away from home.

I don't know where home is
Grandfather.

Evening

for my grandfather

The stork returns from the river
With a snake in its beak –

Wing-shadow and wing-flap and then
He stands on one foot in his tree.

The hens go slowly blind and head to sleep,
Quinces light up crepuscular

And I am old enough to come looking for you
In the back garden at the stove, amid fireflies.

Dinner is always a formal affair with you:
Dark suit, white shirt and tie,

Walnut-oil in your hair.
So you sweat under August

And under your black hat. Your old hands
Tame a fire of twigs and cornstalks.

I imagine you in a painting – tall at the stove
In the garden; fire, polenta

Settled in simmer, eggs, milk in froth –
Framed by a purple sky and rows of quinces.

You stand next to a tree with a stork at the top.
I step into the canvas, a child with uncombed hair,

To stand in the dirt next to you:
A dusty statue with the bluest eyes.

January, Holywell Cemetery

So I walked in, bored with street-noise,
Looking for a place to sit. One

Fallen stone cross among graves
And gravestones, its head on the path,

Brought your voice into my head:
'Someone has to steady your cross

Long after you've gone – that's the other side
Of forgetting; it means you loved.'

But here and now I see that from
The ribs of the forgotten grave

A thick patch of snowdrops
Sways in the mind of the wind and

Where the cross uprooted itself, stray
Crocuses diddle-daddle in the cold sun.

Oh, yes

Every story starts like this:

That was long ago and far from here,
In a country where the names of these herbs heal –
Pojarnita, sunatoare, flori de tei, romanita –
And where women were called Liliana.

When gypsies played accordions
They turned into colliding winds
At corners of unpaved streets:

Dust, skirts, bells, high heels,
Waists undulated
Between rough hands!

Even the cherries
In the orchard turned envious
As summers grew into burning.

Here, the sound of a street accordion
Starts a slow burning in my face.

Then Lilianas, like ballerinas, froze in dance,
When they looked back at their countries
From the eyes of the planes they first flew.

But I see the *hora* turning in their eyes –
Dust, skirts, bells, high heels –
It all happens when the man below my window
Stretches the accordion in his arms.

And of course you won't believe my story
Of the cherries turning red with envy
At the Sunday dance.

Every true story should end in disbelief:
Just like this one. Call it nostalgia.

For my mother and sister

When she was a child and there was a drought
She dressed the cob of the corn in yellowed leaves,
Made overcoats out of rags to clothe the corn dolls
And threw them in the weakened river,
Then ran along the riverbank with the other children
Chanting prayers for rain.

That was long ago. Last night she remembered the chant
And sang it while she held my hand but I don't
Remember the words now, for one never remembers
Things received abundantly –

'Did it rain?' I asked her. I pictured a girl with brown hair,
She, orphan at three, growing along the river and cornfields.
'I don't know' she said, 'but I liked the magic.'

This morning she left with a suitcase – rain
Fell over the Broad Street all through midday –
She and the other one, my dark-eyed sister,
Who has a touch for driving away the pain
Just like that.

I stood at the window and waved, blessed with their strength
For there and then I could finally say: 'Let health and fortune be
With you. I left you across the seas and you came to me
From the heart of love and gave generously.'
They walked along the current of the empty morning street
Carrying miracles with them.